and still, the Lotus Flower Blooms

a spiritual soul's pathway to
self-confidence and success
by Phoebe Garnsworthy

Also By Phoebe Garnsworthy:
Lost Nowhere: A Journey of Self-Discovery (Vol. 1)
Lost Now Here: The Road to Healing (Vol. 2)
Daily Rituals: Positive Affirmations to Attract Love,
Happiness, and Peace
The Spirit Guides: A Short Novella
Define Me Divine Me: a Poetic Display of Affection

and still, the Lotus Flower Blooms - 1st ed.
ISBN: 978-0-6488396-1-3
Paperback
Copyright © 2019 by **Phoebe Garnsworthy**
Artwork by Hannah Adamaszek

www.PhoebeGarnsworthy.com

Life will be sweet

and your mind will be at peace

if you follow your truth.

Your Higher Self awaits your arrival.

dedication to you

This book is dedicated to you.
To that brave soul within you who refuses to give up.
Keep going. Everything is going to align very soon.

Contents

introduction

Every day we are submerged in the unknown and the only anchor in our day is our intuition, the belief that our Higher Self is guiding us on our path. We hold safety in this knowing. For here we can receive undeniable strength and unshakable confidence to pursue our dreams. But even though we hold our self-love close, there are moments of weaknesses, there are circumstances that break us down. We need to remember that this is all part of the process, our life is forever an inner journey of evolution. We are always being given an invitation to lean into the madness and grow our inner strength.

We are like the lotus flower, and the hardships in our life reflect the mud amidst the water. The lotus flower will always emerge through the mud to rise and honor the sun, pure and perfect with not a scratch of dirt on its petals. And this is how we must look at our life - with a great sense of knowing that we, too, will rise. Even though we endure difficult times, these experiences only assist in our journey of personal growth. And so despite the mud that could potentially taint our soul, despite the opposing challenges that can cause great suffering, despite the power of our own mind sometimes tricking us down into misery. We will rise again as the beautiful and pure loving light energy that we are.

And still, the lotus flower blooms.

and still, the Lotus Flower Blooms

a spiritual soul's pathway to
self-confidence and success
by Phoebe Garnsworthy

i see you

You.
Beautiful, delicate, graceful you.
Stop hiding your gifts to the world.
Stop thinking that life is going against you.
Don't you know how divinely guided you are?
How this world is happening for you, not to you?
That everything happens for a reason?
Yes, it's hard to know why,
and it's hard to continue having patience.
But stay strong, stay balanced, and level headed.
because everything that you want is coming.
And all the beauty in the world will be yours,
when the alignment is right.

find the passion

It starts with an idea...
Envision the dream and
use everything in your power
to make it come true.
Have faith in yourself,
listen to yourself,
love yourself,
and believe in yourself.

i am listening

And the more connected I feel with the Universe
knowing that my life flows harmoniously
from inside me,
the easier it is to understand that it's my own reaction
that determines my emotions, my pleasure, my joy.
The more natural it feels for me
to view my life in a positive outlook.
And from doing so, my life continues to expand
gracefully from the center of my heart,
purring in soft rhythmic movements amidst the
vibrations of energy that surrounds me.
My heart beats effortlessly in alignment with the
divine soul who reigns this body,
as I dance amongst the realms of the seen worlds,
mirroring the pure state of nirvana
that echoes above me.
And my higher self smiles before me, feeling the love
that I hold for all of life around me,
and from this place I rest peacefully,
knowing that I am wonderfully looked after all times.

my fears do not define me

The fear you feel is normal,
but you can't feed it any longer.
Because that's what is keeping you small.
You need to let go of this thought,
this limiting belief so that you can align yourself with
who it is that you need to become.
You need to be your own savior,
your own peacemaker,
your own creator of miracles.
Because the Universe is listening.
But if you're too busy repeating the voice of your fears,
the Universe will start thinking that's what you want.
And is it?

Remember: Every conversation with yourself is a
conversation with the Universe.

unexpected turns

She said she wanted change.
But when it happened
nothing was like she thought it would be...
It was a broken heart,
a shattered dream,
clinging to memories of what once was.
She didn't know that it was exactly
what she asked for.
She didn't know that this was the pathway to
everything she's ever wanted and more.

you are

You are so deeply loved.
You were born for a reason.
You are living for a purpose.
You are here to create
and accomplish great things.
Everything is going to be okay.

… And if for a moment you begin to doubt the hand of
the creator who molded you, get out into nature and
touch the beauty of miraculous life around you.

You will feel the harmonizing energy move through
you, reminding you that everything in your life is
exactly where it needs to be.

Telling you that you are always connected to the
divine light within you, reminding you that the loving
energy in your soul is what creates the entire cosmos
of the Universe around you.

Place your heart on your heart and come back home to
the truth.

blessed

You are beautiful.
You are so incredibly beautiful that you don't even
know how to handle your own gift.
There is something so special within you that no one
else has and no one else will ever have.
But you are wasting this gift away because you refuse
to acknowledge it.
You're refusing to pay attention to the divine offering
you provide to the world.
You keep forgetting that you are magnificent.
That you're a magician who creates miracles.
You're a divine creator of the Universe destined to
create incredible things.
Don't you ever forget it — you hear me?

time waster

The moment I stop doing what I love I am not present. My soul has exited my body and is flying in the unseen worlds. I go about my day mechanically. Doing my hated work to simply pass the time. And when my soul re-enters my body that's exactly what it feels like. I have missed a chapter of my life and to me that is so sad. Because every moment of time should be celebrated and treasured. Every second I am on this Earth I should enjoy my passion and share my creations from my heart. But sometimes it's not always that way, so just know that this isn't forever. Things are changing in your favor and very soon everything you want will be yours.

broken shells

She wasn't weird. She just liked strange things.
She got excited when it rained and she stood outside
for hours, letting the water cleanse her soul and wash
away her troubles.
They used to laugh when she'd pick up broken shells
on the ground.
But she felt more connected to the broken than she did
to the whole.
"Good," she heard a voice inside her say on the day
that she couldn't keep walking
with her head held high.
"We are all broken souls moving through time,
searching for the pieces to make us whole," it said.
"And you are far wiser than those who do not see,
for you are aware, you are searching, and you will find
hope with the stillness of your breath to keep moving.
Don't stop, keep going, keep leaning forward toward
the pulling vibrations of your heartstrings."

relax and rejuvenate

it's okay if you just want to rest today, Light Warrior.
It doesn't mean that you're giving up.
But if for a moment you start putting yourself down,
know that sacred work takes time and patience.
Reflect over your life's journey and
remember, how far you've come.

dreaming

Relax, breathing focus and awareness into each breath.
I count down slowly as I enter the crystal cave, seeing
water, reflecting my emotions.
There is a beautiful white light shining up from the
ocean.
I look into the water.
Who do you see?
I dive through the ocean,
come up to a beach,
and stand on the sand.
I feel the heat down at my toes,
the sun has warmed my skin.
Sit here and stay as long as you need,
breathe in her beauty.
All is going to be okay.

To the lands, the sun and the moon,
I give myself to you,
completely and utterly
in this moment.
exhale.

i believe and receive

I trust that the Universe is guiding me
on the right path.
I believe I am looked after
by my Eternal Spirit always.
Because I know that this Universe is my creation.
So all the experiences are my control,
they're my doing.
I ask for something and it appears.
I just need to keep my eyes open to the synchronicity,
and pay attention to what lessons are unfolding for
me. It's all there for one purpose - to live, experience,
grow strong and become the greatest version of myself
possible. Today is no exception, today I will believe in
miracles and open my heart to receive the gifts of love,
support and guidance.

i reward myself with love

I close my eyes and journey deep within.
Allowing the outside noise to just be.
It exists around me
but it doesn't stir the beauty inside me.
And in this sacred space
is where I choose to nurture myself.
Today, I will focus all my energy into loving myself.
I am wise, strong and capable
of handling anything that comes my way.
I am healthy and calm.
I am a magnet for success.
I am worthy of love, of achieving my dreams.
I accept myself exactly as I am.
I am more than enough.

a feeling of hope

I feel like
I am floating
in between
two lives of
where I am,
and
where I want to be.

she is healing

Breathing through the madness in my head.
The stirring from within, a question of the unknown.
And although I feel like I hold all the answers,
the questions of what is still remains.

A calm breeze lifts me up higher
as the trust of what I want still calls through.
And although I don't know what is happening.
I trust and believe that this is the way too.

And as I surrender into the unknown,
I hear a voice say -
"You will find the truth you are seeking.
Today all your pain will go away.
Today, you are to plant the seeds of your
manifestations into the soil of mystical enchantment.
Come walk with me and hold my hand.
Feel the grains of dirt massage your skin and nurture
love throughout your body."

I surrender into her love.
Feeling weightless, I give everything to her.
My pain, my hurt, my fears.
She is taking them all. And yet she still has the
strength to hold herself and keep giving love to me.
She has the courage to inspire me to keep going and in
her embrace of sweet love I am healed.

Sleep my child if you are tired.
You need to listen to what your heart calls for.

the time has come for you to shine

I know you've been hiding who you really are.
You weren't ready to allow yourself to just BE.
But the time has come.
All your hard work has not gone unnoticed,
and you will be rewarded with a life more magnificent
than your wildest dreams.
But to receive your blessings you have to show us the
real you, you have to start believing that you are
worthy of this life. You have to stop apologizing for
how much magic you hold. Because the world is
waiting to welcome you, and the Universe is ready to
bless you. We are all listening.

i release and let go

Surrender into yourself, my love.
You've been battling wars
within your mind for far too long.
It's time to let go and realign with your heart.
And to remember what it feels like
to be loved by you.

Those barriers you've created - it's all in your mind.
It's just a thought — and you have the power to
choose your thoughts.
It's time to set yourself free.
Surrender into yourself, my love.
And remember what it feels like to be loved by you.

she speaks

"You are brave, beautiful, wild and free, my love.
Nothing in the world could ever change that.
Whenever you feel sad, remember the love you hold
right here in your heart. And I promise I will always
be here to meet you.

This is your home, your innerpeace, your sacred space.
It's your safety with me, forever and ever.
You are never alone my love, my love.
The universe is holding your hand,
guiding your soul and walking you along the
enchanted journey that awaits you."

And so she promised to always visit her heart,
no matter how upset with the world she became.
And she remembered the divine light burning bright
in her chest, holding her,
telling her, everything would be okay.

remember

When there's so much peace
inside your heart
the noise outside doesn't matter.

manifesting my dreams

Please bless me with:
Creative confidence to ignite my goals.
Patience and perseverance to fulfill my dreams.
Inspiration and determination
to implement positive changes into my life.
And peace and harmony as I journey within to
reconnect with the Source of Creation.

alone

She felt lonely sometimes. But it never happened when she was by herself. It was only when she mixed with the wrong kind of crowd. Those groups of people who didn't understand her. And once upon a time she would've tried to fit in. Screamed to be listened to or molded to blend. But now she knew the secret to her happiness was her knowledge of self and pride in who she was. That her uniqueness and difference was to be praised not repressed.

So even though her loneliness was hard at times, it created sweeter rewards during those sacred moments when she could be alone all by herself.

emotional landslide

I know today was hard and you're wondering why is this happening to me... But don't give up now. Because you are on the right path. Yep, this messed up, tear jerking journey is the pathway to your greatest victory. And your angels are watching over you, and guiding along the way. Did you know that? You are never alone. Do you hear me?
You are never alone.

you choose

Moving, flowing, freely.
Breathing, giving, receiving.
The movement of energy is constantly
changing and I am the gatherer,
the transformer and the creator.
I am connected to all the energy
in the world around me.
And that energy is flowing
and touching through me.
I can harness it,
I can create it,
I can abuse it.

waiver

She's bold, yet soft.
Strong minded, yet flexible to change.
Believes that everything in her life
is happening for a reason.
But.. She struggles to find patience when allowing her
life to flow. And sometimes she has difficulty trusting
in the Universe. She sometimes loses faith in what it is
that sparks her soul, and sometimes she forgets what
the voice of her intuition sounds like.
But it's only sometimes.

Because every now and again she gets a glimpse of
who she is. Every so often she steps on the path in
alignment with her Higher Self. And every other day
she recalls all the wisdom that is embedded within her
heart.

And it's those moments of bliss that make all the pain
disappear.

determination

There's no limit to how many times you want to
change. Keep evolving and growing to make yourself
happy.
You might lose friends along the way, but those who
are meant to be in your life will never leave, so don't
worry. Just keep focus on what you want
and don't stop until you get it.

you can control your mind

She feels pressured by the choices in her life,
squashed by the limits of time crashing down upon
her. All the things around her seem to creep up quickly
and before she knows it she is suffocated in her own
thoughts. But before she succumbs to the voices in her
head she realizes what's happening.
And without a moment to lose she focuses on
how to calm herself. Taking deep breaths in and out
she looks around quickly.

She finds 5 things she can see and she names them.
She finds 4 things she can touch and she touches them.
She finds 3 things she can hear
and she listens to their sounds.
She finds 2 things she can smell
and she takes her time to smell them.
And she finds 1 thing she can taste and she tastes it.
Picking up a glass of water she swishes it down
and allows the beauty of the energy to cleanse her
worries.

She has managed to self-soothe successfully
and take back control of her mind.
Every time it happens it gets a little bit easier.
And every time she overcomes it, she realizes,
it's all in her head.
And with a brave face, she smiles, knowing that
maybe the fear will never leave her but that she has
the strength to handle anything that comes her way.

thought

It's easy to worry when things around us change quickly. Perhaps we lose a job, a relationship, or even ourselves. But don't fear, because it's all a part of the grand plan. Things collapse so that something better can be created.

Don't doubt the Universe, she's wiser than you.

okay

Everything in your life was there for a reason.
It was necessary at the time and it won't stop you from
being true to yourself,
from living the life you've always wanted -
unless you allow it to.
Unless you choose for it to.
Because this is you.
This is your truth, your purpose, your divinity.
You are blessed,
you are unique, worthy and very deserving.
Everything is going to be okay.
But you need to believe in this too.

No one knows all the answers.
No one holds all the keys.
We're all just doing the best we can with what we've
got. So enjoy this moment. Enjoy this experience.
You will never have this chance for today again so
why not create something beautiful?

When you love, honor and respect yourself whole
heartedly, you will find no time to listen to the
judgement of others, nor judge others yourself.

she tells me the truth

Constantly fighting against the noise.
I need to know I am moving to a better day.
One that is more aligned
with the person I want to become.
One that fulfills my every need and desire I hold.
There's a secret place within my heart that holds the
answers and when I am quiet
I can hear her speaking to me.
She tells me to be brave, that everything is always
happening in my favor.
That even though things may feel confused
or stagnant that this is right where I need to be.
I ask her how much longer am I to be in misery for?
She answers,
"Until you learn to surrender, love unconditionally
and believe in me."

honoring you

Slowly feeling myself again.
Here and there, bit by bit, I see glimpses of her.
She is happiest when she remembers herself,
when she recalls the little things that make her smile.
The pretty things she collects by her bedside,
sometimes hidden in her drawers, some secrets that
she keeps just for herself.

I'm in a fairytale dream that I don't want to wake up
from. I feel like I am alive and awake and at one with
nature. As one exits another enters.
I don't want to leave, these paradise thoughts of life.
Reality is within my reach.

The sky shines brightly upon me and I think as I close
my eyes. I am a vessel of your love.
Fill me up. Use me as your filter.
I am an alchemist.
Wash your love and light through my body and I will
whisper tears into the ground below.
Together we will sing to mother nature.
Singing her praises with so much love and gratitude.
Together we unite this world with soil and water.

You give everyone a heartbeat, it's only because of
you. If we do not say thank you enough its only
because we cannot understand what a miracle you can
make and the gifts you have given us to create.

holding tight within

Rise above it and let it go.
You are a beautiful shining being
who lights up the whole world.
You don't have time to listen to other peoples
insecurities that they're projecting on to you.
Stay focused on your own goals,
your own inner peace and keep going.

depressive thoughts to healing

You just need to do whatever you can to feel better.
And if that means resting, being calm and at peace
with your mind, then that is what you do.
But know that this moment will not last forever.
And know that with time, everything heals.
You will be at peace again, you will feel better.
But right now, your soul is asking for a little bit of time
to regenerate, to touch the Universal energy from
above, to float amongst the spiritual realm before it
travels back down to Earth, to reality.
But…
Don't let your soul wander for too long,
for it likes being up there.
That's where it belongs.
Remember that this life is only temporary.
You have things to do.
You have places to see and people to meet.
You have a whole life worth living,
and your soul wants to live it!
But today, if you just need a rest, then rest.
And if you just need a little bit of time to yourself.
Then do that.
Do just that.
Everything is going to be fine.
Everything is going to be alright.
Time will heal all.

a place she called home

She found a place that felt warm.
It was a place where she could be soft
without being weak.
Where she could be confident
without being perceived as vain.
It was a place where she belonged.
She had been looking all her life for it,
and then finally, she found it.

time to vibrate higher

She missed who she used to be…
Kept looking back to when she was stronger.
When she was younger, more bold, carefree and wild.
Too many challenges had broken her spirit.
Too many heartaches had pushed her to the ground.
The voice within had disappeared and each day she
was happy if all she did was survive.
But the moment she let go of what was,
what could have been and owned up to what is.
She broke the mould around her mind and realized
that this is what life was all about..
A constant circle of up and down.
A cycle of changing, growing and evolving.
And instead of grieving over her old self,
she realized that she had to keep going.
She was never meant to be who she used to be,
(good, for she didn't recognize that girl anymore).
And this new version of herself that was emerging
would be… Confident, clear-headed, compassionate,
understanding, wise, caring, knowing,
and most importantly aligned with the person she
always wanted to be deep down,
the girl she knew she could be,
the girl she has always been.
Except now she would be more braver
and more beautiful than before.

come inside

You don't have to face the challenges all alone
you know?
Your soul is guiding you along your life path,
the wisdom you seek is buried deep within your heart.

rise up

It's time to put the past down to rest and replace that space with something inspiring, something full of love, something that compliments the person you are becoming.

at your fingertips

And when you begin listening to the cravings from your heart, you'll be rewarded with a life more magnificent than your wildest dreams.

to soothe my soul

I surrender into the present moment
to open this gift of time and use it wisely.
I create my sacred space and journey deep within my
heart center - listening to the callings of my soul.
Here, I dive freely into my passions.
Revealing the truth of what makes me happy.
In this sacred space the noise has disappeared.
The desire to please others has subsided.
I've quietened the voice of fear
by rising high into the vibration of love.
I'm using this time to self-improve, self-reflect
and bring my awareness into a new frequency.
And when the time has come to resurface with the
others I will be a new me, a better version of me.
With plans for the future and happiness in my wings.
There will be magic wherever I walk,
and miracles soon to be hatched.
I am ready. I am patient.
I know that all is as it should be.
For the Universe is looking after me.
And from this place I breathe with ease.
Calm, peace and in love.

pathway

Don't settle for anything less
than what you want -
because you do deserve it and it will come to you.
But first, you need to love yourself.

She closes her eyes and taps into the abundance of the
collective unconscious.
Here she gathers the wisdom to heal her past and see
clarity upon her day.
As she wanders through her life she gives love to those
who will listen.
And just as she gives she lavishly she receives the
same in return
for the world is a reflection of internal herself.

confined within misery

So ready to leave this feeling of stuck-ness,
the thoughts in my head are speaking too loudly.
I can't concentrate, can't focus.
I just keep thinking… *what if I fail?*
Thank God for the trees and the leaves
and nature.
It's just what I need.
Her healing kiss,
the strength of her blessings to soothe my soul.
I am not at peace.
I am in chaos and yet the world is silent around me.
While I soak within my wound.
Burning myself internally within.
Denying the voice that calls out in my heart
because I am keeping the others safe.
Because I'm scared to stand out.
But what about me?
When will I let myself breathe?

the mirage

A thorn pricks my finger and my body bleeds red.
But it's a relief, for it shows me that I'm still alive.
The numbness of pain pushes my mind through my chest
stopping my movement and weighing me down low.
I feel sadness and hate at the same time.
Needy and resentment, isolation and fear.
Too many emotions and yet none at all.
"This moment will pass my friend."
I hear a voice from within speak out loud.
But my mind is taking over
and the voice in my heart is hard to be found.
"You will grow and stand tall once again."
It tries once more.
But I'm looking at the ground and I believe in nothing no more.
I pray for this sadness to pass.
Yet I fall back into it too easily,
allowing the waves of anguish to take over my breath.
As I jump right down below into my depth.
And I look at my world through the mirage I've placed upon my vision.
Thinking and believing and wondering.
What is real?

no other option

If you aren't doing what you love
you're insulting your soul.
You're living a lie.
It's time to start nurturing those passions.
The time has come to listen to what's really going
inside. The more we step into alignment with our
hearts desires, the more pleasurable life will become
and the more fulfilled we will feel.
And our life will flow with magnificent beauty.
So, what are you waiting for?

be flexible

When things don't go according to plan
it's because there is a greater pathway
for you to take.
What you want is still coming,
but now, it's actually going to be even better
than you first imagined.
That's crazy, you might think.
And then the Universe laughs.
"Just you wait," she says.

moving through time

Life isn't short.
It's long, because your spirit is eternal,
and so you'll keep repeating the same mistakes,
and keep being challenged with the same situations
until you learn from them, until you heal from them,
until you listen.
If you want to move through this pain and rise to the
next level, accept your reality, be flexible to change and
allow yourself to evolve into who it is that you are
meant to be.
It's all one great big cycle and only you have the
power to lead the way.

praying for answers

She sat beneath the grandmother moon and wept.
"I want meaning from my life," she said.
"I know we're a part of a bigger picture but I don't
know what that picture is. Every challenge keeps
firing at me and some days I don't know if I can take it
any more.
How do I survive?"

The same words kept whispering through her ears,
like soft purrs of mischievous cats. Telling her the truth
that she knew so well.

"Everything in your life is happening for you…"
grandmother moon replied.

"But when will things get easier?"

"When you accept where you are right now, when you
surrender. Then, it will flow."

"But I am, I am, I am." she continued to cry.

"Are you owning your gifts? Are you living your
light? Are your surrounding yourself with the right
vibrations? Are you acting from a place of love and
nurturing your soul?"

She nodded as her tears dried up.
She knew exactly what to do.

growing from the inside

Find the uncomfortable feeling within . . .

Sit with it.
Inhale and exhale.
Ask - "What is it here to teach me."
Listen to the guidance.
Let it go.

Allow something new to be birthed in its place.

manifesting your truth

Your skin is vibrant.
Your body is healthy.
You radiate peaceful energy.
You are glowing with love from the inside out.
Your hard work has paid off
and your passion has brought you wild success.
Your life flows harmoniously
and you are surrounded with blissful happiness.
Your mind is calm and confident.

What do you need to <u>give up today</u> to get 'here'?

self-reliance

We want results and we're willing to do the work,
but we aren't willing to do it consistently.
That means meditating everyday.
That means connecting with source energy everyday.
That means saying 'I love you' to yourself in the
mirror everyday.
We say we want to heal and we want strong
innerpeace, but we don't want to show up and do the
work ... Everyday.
.... But results don't just happen out of nothing.
So when you're ready to step out of the victimizing
child of - 'poor me'
then those results you've always wanted
will be ready for you.
But you need to show up, every day.
And take control of your life.
No one is going to do it for you.
No one.
Not even God.

an opening of truth

These dark times might make you feel lost,
but know that lightness is coming.
The pathway will become apparent soon.
Your hardship isn't for nothing.
It's necessary to push you back on track,
to align you with your true life purpose.
Keep going, be gentle.
And allow life to flow through you.

knowing the light

She wanted to give up.
She felt tired of feeling tired..
of feeling confused…
of not knowing her place..
of believing the world was against her.
And she stared at the ocean before her now ready to surrender. Ready to give in, give up.
The waves crashed violently, tossing and turning into each other in a dramatic mess. It swirled with darkness, with madness, yet glimmered softly with bubbles of light.
It mirrored the chaos in her mind.
And with one last breath she entered the water, but to her surprise, her soul sang with joy. Her mind and body rebalanced itself, soothed its worries from the nurturing love as she swam inside the womb of Mother Earth.
And as she exited the water she felt an immense sensation of calmness, of knowing, with clarity in her vision.
She had re-birthed with strength, with confidence and peace. And the sounds of affirmations spoke sweetly in her mind. They said -
"I am one with the Universe, I am the creator of my life, I am worthy of love, I have all the power to achieve my dreams. I have everything that I need right now. I am in alignment with my destiny. I am alive."

shadow self

Making a noise in this world requires you to have
thick skin. No longer does everyone want to live in
harmony with peace, people would rather see you
burn and fail than rise up high with you.
So many feelings of inadequacy, jealousy and hate
ruining our relationships. Closed-minded people
unaware of their ignorance, unaware of their prejudice
nature. Too much talking without thinking. Too much
blurting out their own trauma and shifting blame.
When are we going to wake up and realize that we are
to unite as one if we want the world to be a better
place?
When will we realize that the true evils are greed and
money? We praise those who don't deserve it and
cower before their command. Too lazy to think for
ourselves. Too stupid to educate and learn the truth.
You think that your words are going to change
something? Change yourself and then watch what
happens.

walking into fate

The longer you spend swimming in your pool of fear,
the harder it will be to get out.
The water will feel warmer, with boring safety,
and the outside will appear to be colder too.
But the moment you decide to leap with faith into the
mystery of new beginnings, not only will the Universe
catch you, but you'll be raised so high that you will
start to fly with new breath and new wings while you
live out your dreams full of magic and beauty as you
have always been destined to do.

present within

This exhaustion that you feel is a calling from within
to reconnect to your internal self.
Today, take some time to just BE.
Breathe in the peace around you.
Surrender to the changes that flow into your life.
Be aware of the signs that are being presented to you.
Move through your space mindfully.
In order to be magnificent you must first master being
still, and this is done by harnessing your spiritual
energy to replenish, rejuvenate and revive.

a place of safety

If ever you are feeling uneasy take a moment and
bring your awareness back into your heart center.
Pay attention to your breath as it flows
gracefully in and out of your body.
This energy is the connection between your inner and
outer worlds. It's harmonizing the space between your
mind, body and soul.
Anchor your soul into the present moment as you
allow your breath to feed a love song into your heart.
And if for a moment you ever feel alone, envision that
light within your soul that breathes love amidst chaos.
That echoes loves when silence persists.
That gives love regardless of any love ever being
returned.
You are love. You are love. You are love.

let me grow

To grow
we must water ourselves.
What do you think tears are for?

her home

She places her hand heavy over her heart
and says quietly to herself, "It's time to remember."
But her mind is sad and keeps turning away.
"Shh," she says again. "You have to remember."

And as the words implied the simplistic truth she
knew,
she cleared her thoughts
and journeyed deep down within.
She found the flame of light that illuminated her soul
and breathed love notes and words of hope to begin.

Then she spoke the love she needed to hear that day -
Because no one else was going to do it for her.
And the moment she did she felt the strength that she
craved. As she invoked the wisdom that had always
laid before her.

The words that she said were nothing new or unheard,
but it was raw and just what she needed.
"You are brave, beautiful and safe," she had said,
And just like that, the energy had freed her.

time for change

The old way of life doesn't fit me anymore.
I'm done with seeking outside for what can only be
fulfilled internally.
From today on I choose to listen to my own needs.
I choose to adapt a healthy routine that sparks
excitement within me. I will nurture my passions with
the same loving care that I would another's. And I will
heed my body's wishes for a soul-nurturing lifestyle
with both rest and rewards. It's a matter of finding the
perfect balance to satisfy my own spiritual harmony. I
cannot rely on another, I cannot wish it were any other
way.
I must utilize the life I have been given and live with a
grateful heart every day.

soothe your soul

Forward.
It was the only way she could go.
Her old life didn't fit anymore.
It was time to leave the past behind.
No more putting herself second.
No more limiting beliefs.
From now on she would walk
as the goddess she was meant to.
And love freely and live without fear.
And go to sleep every night feeling peace within her
heart knowing she was listening to the Universe and
allowing happiness to bloom.

beyond powerful

This is your world.
You have the power to choose your mindset
as you face each challenge that comes your way.
You can believe that everything is working against
you, or know that everything is happening for you.
On those days where you feel less than perfect,
when you feel like life is testing you.
Lean in a little deeper to that sacred space within your
heart and arise to the challenge.
You have the strength to overcome anything
that comes your way.
Because you have the power to be whoever you wish
to be, to achieve whatever dreams you want to pursue.
Life is what you make it, and what you make it,
is up to you.

your wound is your power

The time has come for you to rise again.
Be thankful for your battles but do not let your scars
define you. They were merely a tool to show you how
powerful you can be.

architect of fate

I am the creator of my life,
I choose to align myself with positive vibrations.
I listen to the signs around me,
welcoming change with gratitude.
I know that everything that happens to me
is creating a better life for me.
Because I am surrounded with love at all times.
I am always supported by the Universe.
For we are the same, both the creator and the created.
And together, we welcome each day with an open
heart.

i decide

With every inhale she enters deeper into the magic of
the Universe as the veil to the spirit world lies thin.
And it's in this space that she feels the truth within
her, as she witnesses her Divine Soul dance
through the fabrics of time.
For she is the creator, the mother, the lover.
And she holds the key to bring miracles into her life.

how to heal the world

Love yourself to create innerpeace.
Love your family to encourage trust and unity.
Establish boundaries to protect your energy.
Nurture your passions to fulfill your life.
Eat vegan to save the planet.
Meditate daily to gain clarity.
Educate yourself to eliminate toxic presidencies.
Make your smile your best friend to share connections
with strangers

intuitive calling

You hold the answer to every question you ask.
You can look outside for guidance, but ultimately it
will always bring you back into yourself.

mermaid splashes

Whenever her heart began to weep she would throw
herself carelessly into the wild sea.
The rough currents soothed the chaos she felt inside.
It erased the pain, and cleansed her mind.
Only the sand knew of her true troubles,
only the depth of the unknown could feed her the
light.
And on those days she felt like she couldn't go on,
she tumbled down deeper,
allowing the water to rebirth her.
And when her tears had cried all they could, when the
water washed away her shame she would exit the sea
just as she entered, still a Queen, still a Goddess, but
now, she held a new crown.

the time has come

You act like you're a stranger in a foreign land,
yet you forget that you are made of the Earth,
the stars and the moon.
You are the creator of this world that you walk
soundly upon and now is your time to rise up and
claim your space here on Earth.
Be confident in your decisions, be graceful in your
actions and kind with your words.
You hold so much love inside of you,
don't shut that off from one bad experience.
That experience was there to challenge you,
to drive fire to your heart and burn fury to your being.
You needed to be pushed onto your real life path,
to your true life path and now is your time to step into
the greatness of who you really are and prove you are
hungry.
We've been waiting for you to arrive.
Welcome.

full moon prayer

I harness the energy of this full moon and pray for
guidance to achieve my dreams.
I surrender whole heartedly into your love
and trust that all my needs are being
wonderfully met at all times.
I am ready to receive
the abundance of blessings that are waiting for me.
And with your support by my side, I manifest my
goals, my dreams and my visions into fruition.
With an open heart I speak with clarity.
And I honor my space, my peace and divinity.
I move in alignment with the harmonious vibrations of
the Universe.
With you by my side, I can accomplish anything I set
my mind to.
I know you are with me always.
And so I thank you.

i am confident

She wondered what life would be like if she didn't
hold herself back.
If she allowed her confidence to take control.
Because if she wasn't doing what she loved,
the only other option was to suffer,
to scream and cry at how unfair the world was.
But she couldn't play the victim anymore.
She had to start believing in herself.
I am good enough.
I am worthy of love and great things.
Miracles and magic are coming to me.
I set the rules, I choose my destiny.
Today, I make positive changes and new habits
that support the life I want to live.
And as she confirmed her desires with the Universe,
her higher self watched over and smiled and nodded.
"Finally," she said.

words of warriors

We are strong enough to battle
our own minds.
We just need to believe it.

self soothing

Deep breaths are my savior...
Aroused within my own senses
I seek liberation within.
And the vibrations of my heart are singing loudly.
Guiding me on my life, pushing me forward
toward my destiny.
Every step I take is in my greatest favor.
Every sign I encounter is a blessing from above.
The way of the warrior is laid out before me.
and all I feel,
all I see,
all I know
is clarity, calmness and love.

words of freedom

I'm feeling a deep inner calling to realign to the truth
within my heart.
A desire to decorate the temple of love
around my soul.
My body is craving a moment of praise.
A secret space in my heart.
But I've been ignoring its beauty for far too long.
Today I promise to give myself
the love that I deserve.
I move my body and release old energy.
I heal my organs with nutritious food
from the ground.
I stretch my limbs
and open my heart to embrace the new world.
I breathe sweet love notes to my soul
as I embody the calling from afar…
(the unseen worlds).
The place where my destiny is written.
The more in alignment my heart beats with you there,
the greater my love will feel.
And with one deep breath
I enter a state of mediative bliss,
speaking with the spirits amongst the angelic realm,
Telling me the truth
about what it is that I need to know.
Psst. They say, keep going.

remember the truth

You are perfect
exactly the way you are.
You are beautiful and talented
and no one can ever take that away from you.
You are worthy of miracles to bless your life.
You are loved, irreplaceable.
You are enough.

a choice of love

There's a little voice in my head making up stories.
Pretending. Lying to me. Why am I believing it?
Why am I my own worst energy?
Why am I self-sabotaging?
I let go of the lies I tell myself
and I release all the limiting beliefs
and thoughts that do me no good.
I move through this space into a state of
understanding,
of self-acceptance, of self-respect, self-love and self-
care.
Each day I have a choice of who to listen to and which
side to choose.
And today, I choose love.

the understanding of freedom

In the sacred space between me and the moon
I whisper the true desires of my heart.
And I turn to the crystals in my hands,
feeling their energy vibrate,
seeking the love and comfort from the moon,
as my soul regenerates.
My energy is cleansed as I am gifted the strength to
carry on and face a new day.
And with gratitude I accept the blessings of the
Universe as I feel her support
with an abundance of love.

Over time I have managed to overcome each fear,
each doubt, each weakness.
I have grown resilient from my years;
and courageous and confident.
And it's because of my scars that such triumphs could
occur and so I thank them and I thank you.
If it wasn't for that pain I wouldn't be who I am today.
A strong, blazing flame of light who lives in alignment
with her divine truth.

the recipe

Success begins with self-love.
Listen to your soul speaking to you through your
intuition.
It's there to guide you.
To provide comfort and safety in times of despair.
And if you choose not to listen to it, the only person
you are hurting is yourself.

flow with the rivers of time

You are safe.
You are loved.
You are protected.
The divine hand of creation is always guiding you
along the right path to bring you forth the most
rewarding experiences.
There is no such thing as a wrong way, a wrong choice.
We are here to learn, to unlearn, to relearn.
Have faith in yourself and listen to your intuition.
You know the way forward.
You are never alone.
You have the confidence, strength and courage to
overcome any challenge that comes your way.
You are blessed.
You are loved.
You are in harmony with vibrations of the Universe.
Keep saying it until you believe it.

wise warrior

The time has come for you to rise again.
Be thankful for your battles
but do not let your scars define you.
They were merely a tool to show you how powerful
you can be.

i am one with the universe

That emptiness you feel?
It's a lack of love you have for yourself.
It's an absence of honor, of praise
and celebration of your eternal soul within.
When did you forget to listen to your heart?
When did you stop dancing in the wild?
It's time to sing loudly, stand upon the dirt
and ground your soul back into your body.
Embrace this life, this moment.
You are the most beautiful you have ever been right
now because you are alive.
It's time to start living.

Step forth with confidence, boldly towards your
dreams.

open your eyes

She felt like she never quite fitted in.
Always on the outskirts,
thinking differently to those in the circle.
The things they held importance to didn't hold the
same weight to her
and she wondered if she would ever find another she
could connect with.
She stood out within the crowd, yet felt invisible.
And she wandered through the streets,
bored with life.
She was restless.
Tired of waiting and
searching for that person to hold her hand.
She had had enough.
And of course, that's when it happened.
The moment she had finally let go of wanting
was the day that it came knocking.
Only the strange thing was,
it was in front of her, all along.

the mad truth

She moved through her life often wondering if this is all there is? She kept searching for meaning in the chaos, for the signs in her surroundings. And always looking for the answers within her dreams.

She was living a life of fiction yet craved fantasy and magic. But it all seemed so dull as to what her life could really be.

Where was the helping hand to answer all her prayers? Where was this God she was told to believe would bless her life?

And with a heart full of hope she prayed for change, understanding and peace. And never gave up, and continued to believe that her inner voice would bring her home. And with a thirst for knowledge, the wisdom finally came, but it wasn't the advice she had been seeking all along.

The truth was the lesson that needed to be heard. Her reaction was where the answers had been found. And the safety and clarity she craved, oh so bad, was the ability to let go, to surrender from the life she thought that she was meant to have had.

i surrender with faith

Transformation is woven through our life path.
There's no way to avoid it.
There's no easy option to bypass it.
We need to lean into it, we need to journey through it,
to allow the growth to happen.
If ever you feel out of place, uneasy,
confused as to what the next step is.
Know that the transformation is happening.
Have faith that the answers will come to you
at the right time.
Because everything is always working in your favor.
For the Universe is always supporting
the evolution of your greatest good.
You are shifting, aligning into the person
you need to become.
This is all a part of the process.
Trust. Believe.
Trust. Release.
Trust. Breathe.

gratitude attracts more

I truly believe that you are blessed right in this
moment.
Everything that you need, you already have.
And the things that you want are coming too, but
perhaps they are taking a little while longer for a
reason, or maybe something even better is coming to
you. Have faith and know that it is coming. And shift
your mindset to see the beautiful blessings that are
around you right now.

the promise

I watched her from afar.
Not with jealousy, but admiration.
I felt as though she was dancing amongst the realm of
the unconsciousness, breathing through the seed of life
knowing her spirit is eternal.
Her toes dipped back and forth between reality and
make believe, and from this space she created magic
and miracles, inspiring all who walked alongside her
path.

I know I can join her, dancing right with her.
Not stealing the spotlight, but having my own
moment, living my own life, praising my own glory.
There is enough love for everyone to share.
There is an abundance of praise, of rejoicing, of
success,
of talent for everyone.
We are here to be together. To share. To join. To love.
Just looking at her, she inspired me.
And from now on, I promised I would listen to my
heart.

the ride

There's some days we go through life feeling
unstoppable, invincible, aligned and on top of the
world.

And other days you wish that the Earth would open
up and swallow you whole.

It's difficult living high to low, low to high. You want
answers, you want consistency, you want truth.

But this is life. This is why we live - to feel emotions,
experiences, triumphs, sadness.

So the next time life hands you a card you aren't
prepared for, look internally to solve the puzzle or
breathe deeply to provide yourself patience. Whatever
the problem - you hold the answer.

We just need to breathe and trust and live.

your time is now

You have the strength and confidence to become the best version of yourself that you can be.
It's time to stop making excuses, stop playing the victim and start owning up to your responsibilities.
You're not in competition with anyone other than yourself.
And your time has come to win the race.

the future of now

The day of reckoning is upon us.
No longer can we carry on with outdated ideas,
false promises or lies.
No longer will one person prevail and tower over
another.
No longer will ignorance be tolerated.
But in order for healing to take place everything must
be revealed, everything must be destroyed
in order for rebirth.
And this tragedy we face is enabling us to start afresh
to unify together in order to create the world we have
always wanted.

It's the end of corruption and greed.
Our leaders must now be transparent.
For we are connected together, you, me, the land, the
animals and we must fight as one.

But first we must act by creating changes in our life
that supports our future.
We cannot live just for the day, we must think about
the generations who come after us.
We cannot look back upon this time and tell our
children that we did nothing.

decisions for my future

At every moment we are faced with two options:
One) fear of the unknown, belief that everything is
against me.
Or two) I am in alignment with the path of my destiny,
the wisdom of the Universe is greater than my own
understanding and all is happening according to the
divine time.
I am loved and supported always.

i am safe

She felt as though she didn't belong anywhere.
Constantly moving between places,
searching for somewhere she could call her home.
And every time she entered feeling hopeful
something would push her back down.
Making her think that loneliness
was all she would ever know.
She cried to heal the emptiness within
as she buried her head deeply into her hands.
Everything around her always collapsed with a bang
and she was so tired of picking herself back up.

But all of a sudden something changed in her mind.
The realization that she had been screaming
victimizing cries.
For if she wanted her life to be different there was no
one else, only herself who could save her.
And on this day she promised to be the change she
wished to find, and fed herself words of
encouragement inside her wounds.
She lathered her skin with sweet loving prayers.
And told herself that she was beautiful and loved and
incredible within.
And just like that her whole world changed.
She could see beauty and magic that was never there
before. Only the funny thing was it had always
existed, but she was just too focused on what she
lacked, too focused on what was wrong.
She never thought that maybe everything was perfect,
everything was right where it needed to be, all along.

and so it is

There is more love to be felt amidst the vortex of life.
More wisdom to be learned.
More pain to move through.
More growth to be endured.
But do not be scared
for your sword and shield is strong my light warrior.
You are supported by the gods and goddesses amidst
the realms.
You are supported by so much more than what is
believed to reside beyond the invisible eye.
There is a new world waiting for you.
Open your heart to receive its blessings.

together we rise

As you walk your truth
you'll encourage others to do the same.
And by sharing this love, which illuminates your Soul,
you'll create peace in the world
For your passion will blaze harmoniously from your
heart, connecting with one another.
Rising each other up, we will conquer the world
together.
Vibrating higher, ascending beyond measures.
Forever exploring, forever playing.
Forever praising this light within our hearts.
Let it breathe,
let it sing,
let it live.

the wisdom within

The cool breeze upon her skin makes her feel alive.
The smell of nature in the air soothes her soul and as
she closes her eyes she ventures deep within, entering
the divine beauty that dances inside her.
She knows what it is she must do.
She knows all the words that she has to say.
Now is the time.
Today is the chance she's been waiting for.
She dives blindly into the unknown
yet it's the safest risk she's ever taken.
For she knows the Universe is supporting her,
rooting for her and caring for her.
It's all Love that surrounds her.
It's all Love that's within her.
And from this space, anything is possible.

the night sky

The time has come for you to burn bright.
There's no need to apologize for the darkness nor the
light. Just absorb, acknowledge and allow life to flow
through you. Embody the depths of your emotions,
feel the exchange of power and then dismiss it,
learn how to stand back up. For this sadness is not
here to stay.
Sometimes we need to be completely consumed by the
dark so that an incredible star can be born and that star
is you.

The voice in your heart is your own inner guide.
There is no one else who can tell you what to do,
or give you the advice that you need to hear.
If you are ready to shift your life into the alignment
that you deserve, then listen to the voice within -
it will tell you exactly what it is that your soul craves.

a curious mind

Today, I open myself up to wonder.
As I allow life to flow around me with ease.
I choose which energy frequency I want to reside in,
and here is where I make my plans.
Adapting my body and mind
to understand the world around me.
Changing my habits and lifestyle to align with who I
am and not what society pressures me to be.
I know I am doing the best that I can.
I know that I am acting
according to my level of awareness.
Every day I get stronger and more aware of my
boundaries, my needs and my goals.
And with each understanding comes acceptance with
where I currently am and excitement
for where it is that I want to be.
With time, dedication and practice,
I know that I will get there.

never again

If we ignore the voice from our heart's calling,
we will forget ourselves,
and be swept into the crowd of another's dream.

all is as it should be

At no point is our inner-work complete.
We are forever the student.
We are forever learning off one another.
Anyone who acts righteous to be above someone else
has the greatest growth to go through.
But that's their journey to take, not yours.
Don't let another's insecurity
and self-doubt rub off on you.
Don't buy into another person's limiting beliefs that
it's not possible to live a life full of success and
happiness.
Love is coming to you.
Your manifestations will soon become real.
Keep learning, staying flexible, and open your heart to
listen to the secrets of the Universe because you are
always being guided to fulfill the wonderful life you
are destined to live.
Better days are coming.

it could be simple

The problem keeps circling my mind
unable to be released.
I'm holding onto it tightly.
No one else is holding it but me.
But why?
It's keeping me small and stalling my ability to grow.
By believing this lie I'm holding myself back
from what it is that's real.
I'm choosing to jump to the other side.
Viewing my problems in a different light.
It's done. I tell myself.
Let it go. I scream.
Okay. I reply.
I take a deep breath, exhale the madness.
And just like that, it's gone.

eyes closed

Swish swish swish.
The wind blows through the trees.
Whispering my secrets in my ears and taunting me.
But its not true. Its simply not true.
I'm chasing the side of fear.
I'm running after false hopes and shattered dreams.
I'm forgetting how to open my heart,
Forgetting how to connect with my soul.
I know how, I'm just choosing not to.
But why, when the only person I'm hurting is me.

heart full

I dug a hole in the dirt and buried my sins.
Spitting out the garbage that I held in my head.
The mother Earth swallowed it down and didn't
budge one bit and continued to open her heart to love
me and heal me.
I turned away scared.
Wondering whether I was worthy of such dreams.
And I jumped deep inside the hole that mirrored the
emptiness in my heart.
She filled that space with so much love and
told me I was allowed to create the life that I wanted.
There was no room for self-doubt, for lack of worth, or
limiting beliefs.
And in that space I grew into greatness.

she bleeds

Yes she was hurt, yes she felt pain.
But it was just what she needed.
Because she wasn't putting herself first,
she wasn't honoring herself with love and respect.
And so, the world would keep being cruel
until she listened.
It wasn't until she finally chose to love herself
unconditionally that nothing could harm her anymore,
and from this day on -
she lived happily ever after.

hold space

She needed someone to hold space for her.
She didn't need to be told what to do or be shown
where she went wrong. She just needed to be held in a
space of infinite love and support while she figured it
out on her own. But there was no one there to do that
for her and so, she had no other option than to learn
how to do it for herself.

the past is over

She shared her story with strength, and reflected on
the negative in a positive light. And above all, no tears
came to the surface. She had made peace with her past,
let it go, and something wonderful had moved
through
into its place.
She knew it was all meant to happen.
She knew it was all for a greater cause.
She had healed and life was once again the miraculous
adventure that she knew it always was.
She had just forgotten for a little while.

meditative trance

Time stands still.
I wake up to the new day but it feels the same as
before.
I can rely on only myself to create my happiness, and
with this thought, I begin my routine of self-honoring.
With sleepy eyes I walk to my sacred altar, light a
candle and breathe.
Deep breaths. In and out gently reminding myself that
all is as it should be.
My eyes close to enter the unseen worlds
as I journey deep within.
Traveling within my heart I follow the bright light up
above to the cosmos to join my Higher Self.
She hugs me, holds my hand and tells me.
"All is as it should be."
I open myself to feel the love surrounding me,
to feel the magic of the Universe within me and here,
I sit a little while. Holding hands and rejoicing for life.
I thank the spirits for their blessings and feel the love
within my soul,
then I come back down into my body, open my eyes
and start my day.

secrets shared

A moment of stillness is upon me.
A breath of fresh air,
an invitation to reveal my hidden desires.
An invitation to discover more
of what makes my heart sing.
And I enter the gateway of the unknown with total
freedom,
no worries, no fear.
Just peace and excitement to feel nourished again.
I foresee my dreams and now I walk boldly through
the gate of non-resistance, and enter wholeheartedly
into a space of love, of utter bliss.
I feel my guides by my side, my angels above me as
my soul dances in circles around the divine realm
of the unseen.
I learn the truth about my soul's greatest lessons;
my existence
The truth about life, of the world,
and all there is is to come.

i am strong

It's time to take back your power.
It's time to align with the true talent of your essence.
You are the architect of your life.
You are the creator of your world.
You have the power to ignite the change that you
want,
to achieve the success that you desire - whether that be
a personal or professional goal,
a wish to find true love or to create a family.
Whatever it may be, write those plans up high into the
stars and ask for its blessings.
Now is the time.
The Universe is always listening.

i am courageous

She woke up and decided that from now on
things were going to be different.
No longer would she allow her fears
to hold the reigns on her heart.
She broke out of the cage she built around her soul
and started to walk in alignment with her Higher Self.
She felt the confidence and courage stirring inside her
as the voice of her intuition sang loudly within.
Never again would she dismiss that guidance for
another.
Never again would she lower herself down to fit in.
She was wild and free and at peace with her scars.
She hadn't lost time, it all happened for a reason.
And for the first time in a long time she smiled,
knowing that everything she's ever wanted was right
at her fingertips just waiting for her to shift her mind
to see it clearly for what it was.

sacred space within my heart

I am a divine soul within a magnificent body.
I have the courage, confidence and ability to achieve
my dreams, to be anyone who I want to be.
I am perfect, exactly as I am.
This is my sacred space.

playground

I am a child of the Universe and the world is my
playground.
My life flows in perfect harmony,
in alignment with the divine time.
There is an abundance of love that surrounds me
and grows from within me.
From this space I live with peace and share these
blessings with those who walk beside me in my life.
I turn to the Earth to learn all the wisdom
that I need to know about my time here.
And I journey to the unseen worlds, to the spiritual
realm and heed all the knowledge from the ancestors
who've passed.
I am forever learning and evolving
as I live my life here,
and I am enjoying my experience with an open mind,
with a lighthearted tone, with all the wondrous joy
that beats loudly from within my heart.

release and let go

High above the clouds I fly.
Untouchable invincible.
Soaring through my dreams.
Every wish is granted.
Every question answered.
I am wonderfully looked after by myself.

i am ready

Excited. Ready for challenges.
Eager to see in what direction my life will flow.
My manifestations are written.
My heart is open.
Life is beautiful.
Happiness is coming
Success is aligning.
My life is flowing
harmoniously amongst the fabrics of time.

the creative process

Beginning…
So inspired, excited, words and movements
are flowing though me.
I am flowing with the Universe.
I am dancing with my dreams
and achieving the fruit of life.

Reflection... this is not good enough.
I am not good enough.
I suck. This is crap, throw it.

Space, time. Let go.

Come back after awhile...

Oh wow - you are a genius, divine soul.

in another world

You visited me in my dreams last night.
It's been so many years since you have passed,
and yet I always feel you by my side.
You're with me in every step of my journey.
When I ask you for strength you give me blessings.
When I look for answers,
you hand them to me generously.
Your energy is still alive,
and near me even though I cannot see you.
I love you and will never forget you.

i am more than enough

I am a beautiful soul in a divine body.
I hold great respect for myself
and for everyone around me.
Through being me I bring good into the world.
I listen to my body,
my mind, and my Soul.
I have all the answers I need right now,
And I trust that everything
will come to me in the divine time.
I open my heart to truth, change and wisdom,
and I move in ease, with the vibrations of the
Universe.

love shared

I am in alignment with my Higher Self.
I welcome challenges with ease as I go about my day.
I release all that no longer serves me to
open the space for something new to enter my life.
I know that I am divinely looked after by the Universe.
And I spread love to those who pass me by,
for I believe that the more blessings we share,
the more miracles we will receive.
For my world is your world, together, forever.

gracefully me

I am flowing with the Universe.
Dancing amongst my dreams,
creating and inspiring the
world around me.
Love overflows from the center of my being,
as I live in alignment with my Divine Truth.

blissful breaths

I'm creating a life I love.
Everything I want is within my reach.
and everything I need, I already have.
I speak my intentions boldly,
I write my manifestations clearly,
and my soul is thriving from the space I've created.
My days are filled with self-love and self-care.
My evenings are spent honoring the stars
and the moon.
And when I rest my head to sleep
I dream about lands I'm yet to visit,
sharing the memories with people I love
and remembering the wisdom
from those who've passed.

what it feels like to be me

I am resilient and graceful, confident, and brave.
My soul is grounded in my body
as I claim my space here on Earth.
With gratitude I accept life's blessings and surround
myself with only those whom I love and respect.
I walk with clarity, and I open my mind to change.
I honor the divine within me,
and I speak love notes to my soul
through words of affirmations,
dancing and singing joy from my heart.
I am one with the Universe.
I am powerful beyond comprehension.
I feel love.
I am loved.
I am love.

awakening the truth

Forget everything that has happened before…
Erase your mind, emotions, and thoughts.
It never existed.
This feeling is new.
Listen to yourself.
You hold the key,
the answers, and more.
This is your time…
You can do it.
Believe in yourself.
Because no one else will
and no one else matters.
Because, this is your life.
Your reality.
It is the product of your thoughts,
your beliefs and more.

moonlight kisses

I am aligning with the pathway of my Higher Self.
my destiny is at my fingertips.
I can feel the infinite love of the Universe
surrounding me.
Every moment in my life has led me to this point.
Every hurt, every pain, every heartache.
I know the reasons why.
I've built an armor of gold around my heart.
As I surrender completely and trust in the divine.
And I make peace with whatever may come.
For I am stronger than ever before,
more confident, more brave, more fearless.
But I am ready for the world to show me how.
Show me now.
Thank you, my moon, my love.
Thank you.

simple plan for success

She wakes up empowered.
Ready for whatever challenge she was to encounter
that day. She feels confident in her decisions, peaceful
in her surroundings and eager to see what direction
her life would flow. She couldn't help but feel in love
with the world and every living creature around her. It
only meant one thing; she was stepping into alignment
with her Higher Self.
And everything she had ever dreamed of was on its
way to her and everything she had ever wanted was
right within her grasp.
She just needed to be patient and allow the Universe to
pick the timing of her life and while she waited she
just needed to breathe and laugh and love.

unshakable faith in the universe

I trust that my life is unfolding as it is meant to.
I know that I am always supported by Grace
as I fulfill my life purpose.
In this sacred space I am loved in abundance.
I am resilient, strong and capable of handling anything
that comes my way.
I am patient as I go about my day.
Opening my heart to mystery and wonder
I hold love close to my heart
as I heal the pathway of my ancestors,
and reveal the sacredness of my Divine Soul.
She breathes with ease knowing that her life is flowing
in alignment with the Universe.
Knowing that her every move is supported,
nurtured and received.
She walks the chosen path and yet is the one who
creates the path before her.
For she is the creator of her Universe, the divine spirit.
She goes about her day spreading love and joy from
the center of her heart
And she receives that same love in return,
as she surrounds herself with high vibrational people,
a constant flow of energy, giving and receiving.

healing from source

Nature is the answer for every cure possible.
Lie down on the soil and let the ground heal you.

clarity in my mind

How I cannot wait for the sun to shine upon my skin.
To hear the sounds of nature.
To rest my head upon the grass.
The simplest truth of sweet harmony.
Of heavenly grace, of angels breathing.
I feel at peace.
Finally on the right path.
And life is flowing around with ease.
Not a worry in the world.
Not a care in the sky.

patience, my love

I can see my goals so clearly in the horizon.
I know how life will feel the moment they come true.
But I cannot see the process…
I do not know how.
All I know is that it's going to happen.
And with my intentions spoken loudly to the stars and
the moon and with my heart always listening to the
sounds of your song.
I am open, ready and walking my path.
I am moving, swimming and breathing your love
song.

behind the veil

With every exhale
she releases all that no longer serves her.
And with every inhale she harnesses
the energy of the Universe.
What will she do with such power inside?
She will create miracles and magic
as she paints her world with love.
Tapping into the wisdom of her soul,
the home of her inner peace.
Here she sing songs
as she strips herself bare.
Being her own role model,
her own witch, healer and queen.
So many roles. So many players.
She has the power to be whoever she chooses.
And with gratitude, she exhales.
Knowing the truth of who she is,
an architect of making dreams come true.

energetic pulls

There's a whirlwind of energy circulating around me,
within me and before me.
I step boldly into the vortex of your love
and feel the sensations ripple through my soul.
I ignite with you in this moment to connect,
share and release.
You support me, and I support you.
Mirroring, movement, magic,
our voice, our hands, our hearts.
together we heal, hold space, and Love.
Love.
Love.

walking your truth

As you listen to the magical callings of your Soul,
The whole Universe is listening too,
and the path of your destiny is woven,
carefully laid out,
waiting for you.

manifestations

The energy from the moon reveals our thoughts from
the subconscious mind.
And the side of us that we keep hidden breathes,
finally.
It has its time to shine.
The vibrations of the world around
us mirrors this reflection,
and it too, lives with joy, from the center of its heart.

With a whispering hush she invokes our hidden
desires, and with her magical touch
she supports our inner vision.
She gives a miracle just waiting to be revealed.
Remember - whatever you wish you shall receive.

gratitude awaits

My hands are open, ready to receive.
I know my angels are listening to my prayers
as a deep sense of peace surrounds me.
And a love is growing within me.
My life is flourishing exactly as I imagined it would.
With beauty.
With magic.
With miracles.
I am utterly grateful for your blessings.

between silence

All the answers to the questions I seek
are within me.
I just need to silence
my mind and listen.
If I can dream it,
it is possible.

The voice in your Heart is your own Inner Guide.
There is no one else who can tell you what to do,
or give you the advice that you need to hear.
If you are ready to shift your life into the alignment
that you deserve,
then listen to the voice within -
it will tell you exactly what it is that your Soul Craves.

it has begun

There's a tingling sensation vibrating through my
body. It's the knowing that something wonderful has
begun. My challenges are behind me. My past has
healed. I have no regrets. Only happiness within.
I finally feel like I am walking in alignment with my
Higher Self and that life is flowing with ease.
Bringing forth beautiful miracles right into my hands.
I am breathing and living the blessings that surround
me.

i am present

She stood strong.
With warrior blood moving through her veins
She knew the spirits of her ancestors were behind her.
And she moved courageously through her life
despite the combats that she faced,
continuing to spread acts of love and wisdom
to those who were open to receiving it.
Very few knew of the fights she endured,
but all saw the strength that her scars embodied.
Every time she fell, she rose again faster than before,
feeling the support of her divine self within.
Her path would not always be easy,
she knew it couldn't be that way.
For such turmoil had the ability to provide the greatest
depth of love she could ever ask for.
It wasn't a question in her mind if she was to continue
or not, for this was the way of the warrior.

the life i create

Spirituality is my religion.
My temple is my body.
My God is my Higher Self.
And nature is my church.
I sing prayers to the Universe because
I know that my words create my reality.
And with every breath I enter a sacred space
in the unseen worlds where I nurture and give love
back into my soul.

heartfelt

She honors the Divine within.
By loving herself through self-nurturing care.
And her inner-child heals,
as the voice of her Spirit speaks louder.
Every day she becomes more and more herself.
And her Soul thanks her for it,
dancing with grace, harmoniously through life.

fulfill

Everything that I want is coming.
I will be healed.
I will find my soulmate and fall in love.
I will be rewarded for all my hard work.
I will be successful in everything that I do.
I will live a long, healthy, and happy life
and be proud of it.

fulfilled

Everything that you want is coming.
You will be healed.
You will find your soulmate and fall in love.
You will be rewarded for all your hard work.
You will be successful in everything that you do.
You will live a long, healthy, and happy life
and look back and feel proud of it.

the truth beyond words

Your Higher Self knows your life plan to achieve your dreams (the pathway of your destiny). Sometimes we take a bit longer than we'd like but the direction is always the same. And on those days when coincidences occur (synchronicity) it's a push along our path of fate - a reminder that we are looked after and that everything we want is coming.
Don't ignore the signs.

awoken to be me

There comes a moment in your life when everything aligns. When your heart beats differently than it did before. And excitement rushes through your veins as you embark upon a new day, a new journey. One that joins your presence with your soul's greatest desire. You start to feel everything around you with so much more depth than you ever thought possible and with it comes eternal gratitude for your profound understanding, this new way of life.

You feel as though you've just opened your eyes for the very first time, yet you're completely aware that this reality has existed since the beginning. But it's only now that you've deemed yourself worthy, that you've chosen to give yourself the love that you deserve and step up to the life that you've always meant to have been living.

Only now you're living it with more depth, more understanding, more love, more admiration. For you've endured the darkness, you've been on the other side. It's enabled you to have more compassion, more wisdom, more patience, more determination. And now the taste of life is more sweeter than possibly imagined, and love has more layers than you ever thought to exist. And there is a new meaning for what forever can hold.

acceptance granted

Every challenge in our life is an invitation to evolve
into the greatest version of ourselves.

to feed my soul

I close my eyes
and feel the light of my existence inside me.
It's the beginning of creation, the fire within my soul.
And with every deep breath,
this flame inside of me grows bigger, brighter, bolder.
And with every exhale, it releases anything that holds
me back, or that is helping me no more.

I take another deep breath and feel the love in my
heart burning brighter.
It is truth of my beauty,
the sacred space where my soul resides.
And as I exhale,
I let go of any pain or trauma that I once held so close.
I release any versions of myself that I no longer align
with, or whoever it is that I once was.

I take one last deep breath and step closer
to my Higher Self.
I'm feeling grounded in my skin, stronger in my being.
And in this weightless dimension I hear the voice of
my intuition. I feel my energy rejuvenated as I
surrender wholehearted into the wisdom of the
Universe, allowing myself to be held, to be nurtured,
by its infinite love.

clarity through patience

I wake up with energy buzzing through my body,
opening my mind with glimmers of hope about
what I can bring to my day.
And then time changes things and I forget.
I forget how blessed my life is.
How much beauty surrounds me and within me.
I look down wondering when things will change.
Forgetting that it's me who needs to change
the way I look at things.
I'm surrounded with the gift of time to do all the
things I've been dreaming about.
All those skills I wish I knew,
now is my time to learn them.
And the passions that I've been hushing
finally have their moment to shine.
And so that's what I am doing
with this great moment of stillness.
I'm finding myself, I'm living my life.
But now, it's on my terms.
With a clean slate, a new beginning.
Everything I've ever wanted is mine.

i honor myself

My body is my temple
and in this sacred space I speak love notes to my soul
through words of affirmations.
I bring peace to my mind with nurturing vibrations
from the Earth.
And I give harmony to my body by massaging sweet
smelling oils upon my skin.
My body is my temple and I honor and respect this
sacred space everyday.

i have arrived

I finally feel like I am living
the life that I was meant to.
Surrounded by nature and enamored
in the presence of her beauty,
I breathe with gratitude.
Inhaling fresh air to lighten my mind,
as I cleanse my body with the salt water seas,
and kiss my skin with sunshine.
Admiring the miraculous day
gifted from the Universe.
And as nighttime falls I, too, glisten like the stars,
shining my Soul,
I absorb the vibrations of the moon.
And as I sleep,
I rest my head on a pillow of sweet perfume,
healing my body as I dream.
I finally understand that everything is from within.
And I thank you, I love you
for choosing this body,
for living the life I want to live.
Knowing that every choice is mine.

good witch

She was a good witch.
She burned sage to clear the energy,
and palo santo to invite in harmony
as she lathered essential oils upon her skin.
She honored the sun and the moon
as she created rituals beneath the stars.
She praised all living creatures as equal
and would never eat another animal.
She could feel their vibrations too strongly
to absorb them in her being.
She spent her evenings praising the gods and
goddesses
of the Universe,
and in the daytime she honored the divine within.
Gathering her energy within sacred spaces,
she harnessed the wisdom from the ancestors
who had passed.
Some called her crazy.
Others didn't understand.
But it didn't matter.
She knew who she was and that's all that mattered.
She was spreading love.
She was being herself.
And it made her happy.

rhythmic heartbeats

Her energy was inspiring,
the way she danced from within her soul.
It was like the music from the Universe was beating
right through her heart.
"It's within you too,"
she says as she takes your hand to show you,
closing her eyes in deep ecstasy,
inhaling the beauty all around.
You surrender to her command,
flowing in harmony with her grace,
moving your feet,
you listen to the sounds that echo.
And for a moment in time your bodies were no
longer,
the exterior had faded
as you danced together as one.

the one duty

Silence of life strumming gently around me.
If I am still enough I can witness the miracles.
And as I ponder my thoughts, I realize.
Nothing else matters but this world.
This nature of life around us.
It will survive.
We are merely tiny player in the scheme of things,
Yet we believe that we are so much more
because we can think!
Ha!
What good use is thinking if our hearts are not full of
love.
If we neglect the one duty that we are born on this
Earth for and that is to show love, to connect, to unite.
We must come forth with those who need it most.
We must explore life with others who see the dark
We must save each other,
if we are to accomplish anything in this life.
As long as there is kindness and forgiveness and
compassion, then we are doing it right.

following

I live an ethical life.

I respect the decisions of others and this enables us to
live harmoniously in peace.

I know that everyone is trying their hardest, acting
with accordance to their level of awareness and so I
open my heart with love, in the trust that others
will strive to do the same.

spiritual witch

She was a spiritual witch.

She collected crystals from the seaside and bathed her body with salt water kisses. She healed her wounds with the power of plants as she followed the sun around the world, picking flowers and spreading their seeds.

She walked barefoot, living off mother nature's blessings and she hugged trees as she ate their fruit and talked to the animals who walked alongside her. She understood how to use her breath to enter nirvana and from this space, her life flowed in harmony. Her goal was clear and simple: to love and leave the world more beautiful than she found it.

ritual

I call upon the energy of the Earth, the healing
vibrations of mother nature.
Bless me with your energy.
Ground my soul into my body and bring me fluidly
into the present moment.
Here I will lay for a little while.
Long enough until I feel replenished and revitalized.

That's the beauty of the Earth.
No matter how much we take and take
she always has enough love to keep giving.
She takes away our pain and sorrows and replaces that
energy with calm and peace.

I am resilient and graceful, confident, and brave.
My soul is grounded in my body as I claim my
space here on Earth.
With gratitude I accept life's blessings and surround
myself with only those who I love and respect.
I walk with clarity, and I open my mind to change.

my religion

I believe that . . .
You hold the answers to everything you need to know
in your life.
You have the strength to overcome any problem
that comes your way.
You have a soul who is guiding you
along your pathway of life.
You are never alone
because the Universe is always within you.
You are divinely guided by your ancestors.
You are capable of becoming whoever you want to be.
You are beautiful, wild and free.
You are alive and pure hearted.
You are surrounded with love.
You are love.

united together always

Her body awoke to the soothing vibrations from the
Universe.
She felt the beauty of its touch dance within her heart
and with gratitude she listened to the secret songs as
they moved around her sacred space.
With a deep breath in she allowed it to enter,
Revitalizing her soul to be one with the Universe.
She opened herself to flow with the harmony of its
grace, moving her feet as she echoed through the
lands.
Moving slowly, gradually toward the pull of love she
found her homeland.
And for a moment in time they danced together as
one.
Her body was no longer, and she smiled with ease,
knowing that finally she was living in alignment with
her Higher Self.

it's real

And then finally it happened.
She woke up feeling confident
and beautiful in her skin.
She was successful and wise beyond her years.
She was living the life
she had always dreamed about.
She had created a strong relationship with herself
and everyone in her life mirrored
that same connection.
She was at peace with her past, excited for the future,
yet had mastered the skill of living with gratitude in
the present moment.
She breezed through the day harnessing the power
within her.
Embodying the true meaning of living life to the
fullest.
And those who crossed her path were inspired,
honored to be walking alongside such a goddess,
such an angel, she was a blessing for the world in this
moment of time.

today

And from that day on she made a vow:
To put herself first, above everyone and everything.
And she lived happily ever after.

about the author

Phoebe Garnsworthy

Phoebe Garnsworthy is an Australian female author
who seeks to discover magic in everyday life.
She travels between the worlds of the seen and
unseen, gathering ancient wisdom and angelic energy.
Her writings reflect a dance with the mystical and
wonderful, an intoxicating love potion to devour in a
world that overflows with forgotten love and
enchantment.

The intention of her writing is to encourage conscious
living and unconditional love.

www.PhoebeGarnsworthy.com

Made in the USA
Middletown, DE
17 February 2021